No More Midnight Tears

Arketa Williams

No More Midnight Tears

Copyright © 2004 by Arketa Williams

All Rights Reserved.

Reproduction of text in whole or in part without expressed written consent by the author is not permitted and is unlawful according to the 1976 United States Copyright Act.

Printed in the United States of America

Cover Design: Inspired Reflections Graphic Design
irgraphics@hotmail.com

Published in the United States by Pen2Pad Ink Publishing.

Requests to publish work from this book or to contact the author should be sent to: contact@pen2padink.org

Arketa Williams retains the rights to all images

This book has been revised in 2015 and 2018

Acknowledgments

First and foremost, I would like to thank God for blessing me with the ability to express myself creatively and everyone who supported me as I strived to make my dreams come true.

> In memory of my mother
> Shelline Williams
> November 18, 1955-September 10, 1995

To my dad Elijah Williams thank you for all your love, encouragement, finances and continuous support along the way. It was greatly needed and welcomed.

To Joslynn and Tyra, my big sisters, who have gotten up out of their sleep in the midnight hour to listen to my stories, poems and tantrums. Our three-way conversations were both humorous and enlightening. I love you both. Thank you!

To my babies (my nieces, nephews and god children) Elijah, Sarah, Kenneth, Breanna, Angel, Tiana, Airyana, Symonia, Ezell and Sakena thank you for all the laughs, stories and cheers as I rehearsed for poetic concerts and performances. You were the best audience anyone could ever ask for and the most encouraging. Know that everything I do I do in honor of you! I love and no matter where life takes you I'll be there to support you 200%.

To all my spiritual family, thank you for not allowing me to quit and throw in the towel when I got too tired to keep pressing on. Thank you for your prayers, wisdom and long conversations to keep me on the right track. As well as all the venting sessions we had. I love you all. Some of you have really been my angels without wings and you know who you are. (Smile)

To my girls, my aces and my closest friends. Erica, Shamora, Iaisha, Porsha, Nisha, Aisha, Gloria, Crystal and Robin we have shared memories, stories, tears and successes. You each hold a different place in my heart but are all equally special to me. Thank you for all your encouragement, time and assistance in a wide variety of dramatic but entertaining situations. I love you all!!!!

To my aunts, uncles and cousin's thanks for all your support. Many of you have been my greatest inspirations. Thank you!!

Contents

1. Check the Gratitude in Your Attitude............................ 10
2. One Woman's Reflection... 13
3. If I Never Try... 15
4. Eat, Sleep, and Breathe Poetry..................................... 18
5. Deeper... 21
6. The Shadows of Reality.. 23
7. Let Go and Let God Do It... 27
8. Feeling Like Trash but Always a Treasure.................... 30
9. Especially for You... 33
10. Incomplete... 35
11. Inside Out.. 36
12. No Name on a New Entry.. 38
13. Misfit... 39
14. Create.. 41
15. One Mind One God... 42
16. A New Creation.. 44
17. Depression... 45
18. What to Do.. 47
19. Where I Live.. 48
20. Down Low... 50
21. My Mind.. 52
22. I Wasn't Assigned to You.. 55

23. I Never Claimed Perfect.. 57
24. Remember This.. 60
25. Shedding the Emptiness.. 64
26. Alone.. 65
27. Broken Promises.. 66

Check the Gratitude in Your Attitude

Is there a time in your life when you subconsciously controversially rehearse to thee?
A false gratitude that crosses the boundaries of greed
And overlaps with your own demented sense of need
As you aimlessly lessen your hopes and dreams
By misdirecting your worship to fulfill other things

Is there a time in your life when God walked you through to your better days?
And your praise evaporated just after the storms went away
Allowing your pains to once again become evident
As thoughts of "why" becomes more relevant

Is there a time in your life when you ungratefully cried out spiritually?
At the rude interruption of your joy and peace
Yet you still stepped out of bed without so much as a thank you
But come back again prostrate in his presence waiting for your turmoil to cease

But what about when the time comes for your mind to make the mastery
To connect the Hypocrisy
Of the gratitude that only comes with your burdens of misery and strife
And God no longer lays hidden in the shadows behind the false pretenses of your life

And He no longer reigns second best while you play with His heartstrings
Realizing your life embodies more than just your being
And your eyes begin to widen with the horizons of unseen now seen
As you walk together in a divine union of thankful rejoicing

Moving past the here and now into the present just to create a future
Re-evaluating the mistakes of the selfishness you now have to suture
While challenging yourself to check the standards of your gratitude
Without becoming confined to the laziness of your attitude.

One Woman's Reflection

I am all of one woman
And it's my own reflection I see
One of truth, wisdom, and love
It is my pure and precious beauty

I am one of an elegant spirit
Of different grace and unique style
One whose unusual flow besets her
Still yet baring the sunset in her smile

There's a gentle peace in my posture
An anointing with the words that's so divine
It makes my first impression everlasting
It makes me one of a kind

I have a unique glide in my steps
I carry a different curve in my hips
Which allows my presence to be known
And my name to gently rest upon your lips

Yes, my image piers a woman or renowned talents
One accompanied by a mighty strength and courage too
Hurdling many obstacles while in a constant warfare
with Satan
Yet by God's grace still triumphing through

It reveals all my shed tears of heartaches
Those that hold the victories as well as the defeats
It peacefully clutches the side of wisdom
That keeps me planted on my feet

It mirrors to me the knocking of love
That I once desperately set out to seek
As it rested inside confusion's shadow
While compromised I tried to keep

It tells the stories of my journey of struggles
Portrayed backwards for me to see
That through just one woman's reflection I must be graceful
At how far down this tangled road I've finally come to be!

If I Never Try

If I never try then I should've gave up yesterday
Because tomorrow's never promised and today's
too far away
And with no dreams for me to reach
There's no voyage for me to share and no sessions
for me to teach
If I Never Try

If I never try I'm left unorganized, tired and still
standing at the cross roads of pity and defeat
Trying to measure up to the expectations set too
high for me to compete
Feeling like I'm not good enough, while attempting
to understand who I'm supposed to be
Left still seeking alternate paths beyond what only
I can see
If I Never Try

If I never try there'll be a series of events that expands
beyond my limitations
That amplifies my horizons while exhaling my hesitation
As my visions now blinded by society's misconceptions
If I Never Try

If I never try my life will become widely diluted
And all the hopes of a prosperous future then become
falsely pursued
As I fall into the same traps as those that proceeded before
And I'll exist just the same, becoming nothing better
amounting to nothing more
If I Never Try

𝔍f I never try my words would never spark the mind of the young man who's supposed to stand as the new millennium rebel for his generation
Or move to reach the heart of the young lady so embraced by the streets that she then becomes twisted by the transformation of a verbal condemnation
If I Never Try

𝔍f I never try I inhibit myself of expressing my unwritten incubations
There by hindering following children of declaring their cerebral in dictations
While enhancing the spoken hallucinations of the proper moral upstanding
Meanwhile magnifying the perception of improper conduct mishandling
If I Never Try

𝔍f I never try then my pen can never touch the pad of change to recreate something new
And I fall frustrated by the abandoned side of love incapable of reaching you
Never rebirthing the darkness of death into the brightness of the life today
After all, if I never try then I should've gave up yesterday
Because tomorrow is never promised and today is too far away

Eat, Sleep, and Breathe Poetry

I eat, sleep, and breathe poetry
It is because of the cerebral incarceration
That I'm able to so freely flow with these lyrical libations
And I write
I write of intensifying thoughts and complex theories
The excruciating webs of deceit that leave my soul weary
I recreate the trials that dwell in me
To the point that only soaring from the ink of my pen can they truly be free
Therefore I eat, sleep, and breathe my poetry

Even in the beginning God did poetry
He said, "let there be" and it was
So here I am asking that you just show some love
Because it is also for you that I write

For bright eyed little girls so picked on and ridiculed that you can't even see your own beauty
Too caught up in the words of others of how you're supposed to be
I write

For wanna be thugged out little boys trying to be like 50cent, Pac, Snoop, and/or Biggie
Those lying in the blindness of stupidity that we're losing to the streets
I write

For the young people attempting to be like

the chics in the videos and you don't desire to wear any clothes
I write to tell you that success lies beyond
UPN and WB
ABC and BET
TNT and HBO
The key of life cannot be found in the latest rap video
And so it is for you that I write

I write to give you a piece of me so that my pains can be your healing
So that my trials can help you start your living
So that the tears that fall from my eyes can reach your soul
And I can inhale your fragmented breaths while reconstructing your incompletes into a whole
I write so that when I open the door to success and opportunity
I can come back to these same ghetto streets and bring many of you through with me
By eating, sleeping, and breathing poetry.

Deeper

I want to go deeper than
Carved sculptures and colored designs
Structured lands and golden rhymes
Nameless children holding darkened dreams
On shattered glass shores clinging by any means
I want to go deeper

I want to go deep than
The souls drowning in the Mississippi
As I attempt to grasp freedom from the clutches that hinder me
While I journey down Niles of crystal dried tear drops
On tinted specks of homeless stops
I want to go deeper

I want to go deeper than
The quivers of your body on moonless nights
Silhouette shadows on extended heights
Crowded cells with shimmers of shame and defeat
The weight of the world that thinks it has me beat
I want to go deeper

I want to go deeper than
Heavens highs and hells lows
Molested children from sanctified halos
False revelations on inked stair wells
Silenced cities and inscribed tales
I want to go deeper

I want to go deeper than
Impressive manifestations of depraved despairs

Deprived endearment and vacant stares
Hollowed Niles of crowded thoughts
A faint glance after a vision sought
I want to go deeper

I want to go deeper than
The electricity running through the power lines
An electrifying orgasm so out of sight it leaves your mind behind
Or mirroring reflection of a soul exchange
So deep it brings your mind, body, and soul on one accord
I want to go deeper.

The Shadows of Reality

For years I created on my canvas an exquisite inspiration spoken words have centered around
And contained within each master piece conveyed a new revelation I found

As I journey back down memory lane of the streets that paved my way
The lifestyles that encouraged my soul as death grew closer each day
Yes, I remember the inspiring alcoholic that sang the blues
And the street pharmacist on my block that reported the news

And the pastor up the street
Entangled in a web of deceit
Worrying about his future cause his mistress is about due
And when his wife found out she liked to kill her and him too

Stressing cause words spread quickly when the gossip's good
Now ducking and running and another funeral's where they stood
Yet another black man imprisoned for life cause revenge he tried to seek
Since the only love we understood was found in these here streets

I remember tearing away her flesh with the blade in my hand

Cat fighting in the streets over sleeping with the same man
While the drug addicted mother o/d's at her children's bedside
And leaves them with daddy who's destroying them on the inside

As they grow up searching holding on to an artificial love desiring for it to be true
Continuously being knocked upside their head and seven fathers later still looking for someone to love you

Watching crack babies being abandoned in the old building behind your home
And challenged infants slaughtered cause the mama couldn't make it on her own
Reminiscing of the younger days when life seemed so black and white
Now all we view is self-destruction seeping through blinding our sight

Battles being fought all over the lands
Decaying the structure of our homes too weakened by our flesh to even take a stand
Starting at the head and working its way down
The president can't even lead by the example of turning things around

Dying for no just cause killing thousands in one day
Twin towers falling, pentagons burning, bombing countries seeking revenge, attempting to fulfill a debt you cannot pay

Snipers passing head shots with free will convicting

the innocent silencing them for life
Inflicting upon society yet another burden of misery and strife
The world is falling apart with no place for the interjection of someone to make a difference
Now bound and shackled in a new form of captivity you remain planted with no hindrance

Allowing your situations and circumstances to define your futures outcome
Laying in the laziness of your mind so tangled in corruption you enable yourself to succeed
Because the streets have taken control of the things you truly need
Families abandoning one another running after a temporary relief at your highest peak
As our people face the real reality of living life in society's streets.

Let Go and Let God Do It

Passing time I watch you gracefully gliding across the room
Swinging and swaying rotating your hips to the sweetest melody
I sit in an awe of admiration wishing it were me

Out of this chair I'd love to leap
But confined to this seat there's a secret I must keep
Shattered and shaken, torn and tiered
Dangerously unloading the pains I bare
Now in the midst of a storm this vision appears
And all of a sudden these voices I hear
An angel embraces me and holds me close
As I now stand shedding tears at the things that hurt me most
I would love to be like you and walk with Jesus as my guide
I know I see Him standing there with his arms stretched open wide
I know I hear Him calling me, yelling out my name
And that once I fall in love with Him things will never be the same

But you don't know the roads I've traveled, the places I've been, and the things I've seen
You don't know who I am and how I got so evil and mean
You don't know about my secrets and the scars I have inside
Yes, I do, but as you see His arms are still stretched

open wide

You see He knows about your hurt and all that you've been through
And He's still making an attempt to walk with you
He saw you struggling and fighting your way through life
He cried for you as you held in all your misery and strife

Now He's asking you to allow Him to be the one to wash away the pains of your past
And allow Him to show you a love that will continuously last
Allow Him to comfort you as you baptize your pillows in mid-night tears
Allow Him to wipe away the pains of yester-years

Allow Him to save you and set you free
Now He's crying out "So my child will you come and walk with me?"

Feeling Like Trash but Always a Treasure

Feeling unworthy you disgracefully attempt to hide your face in shame unable to see His grace and mercy you boggle yourself with blame
Frolicking through life's stumbling blocks like yesterday's trash you see today's news
No way to envision an escape you continuously become misused and abused

Attempting to grasp hold to a concept of a temporary moment's pleasure to stand
Longing for attention, yearning for that warm sensation to fill your hand
Fornicating through the beats of your heart lusting after that missing link
Giving misery so much company you enable yourself to think

Dishonorable feeling the filth piercing the sides of your soul
Desperately seeking to comprehend how his love can make you whole
Always hearing the stories of His miracles being unveiled and people made new
But somehow you've convinced yourself you've made too many mistakes for Him to love you

Satan has you feeling like a failure in a mindset that not even God can help
But even after the drugs and drinks a full deck still

hasn't been dealt
Because God said old things shall pass away and behold I make you new
My love is unconditional despite what you may do

My grace is sufficient and when my blood was shed I washed you whole
I've looked beyond your faults and saw your needs my eyes are the windows of your soul
For I've come that you might have life and have it more abundantly
There's no complex secrets or hidden theory that defines the characteristics of me

All you do is cast all your cares over and surrender yourself there's no cute little
Antidote to the way that lives should be
When I saw you I perceive you as a mother would her child
Longing to be near growing closer all the while

Loving you more and more with the passing of each day
Because you were never trash but always my hidden treasure manifesting along the way.

Especially For You

Spoken words through hateration
Without hesitation
Holding no limitations
Allowing me to spit lyrics just for you

Lines of baffled truths seeing reality
Capturing new identities
Still holding old amenities
Allows me to spit lyrics just for you

Sending my emotions down blackened stairwells
And hollowed roads
Protecting my soul from the stories told
Leaving my life on hold
Allows me to spit these lyrics just for you

Forcing myself to rise above my circumstances
To follow a God of a second chance
Lying behind the Plexiglas which reflects an indescribable glance
Allows me to spit these lyrics just for you

Flying through the firing flames
Of unextinguished pains
Just to find sanity in the midst of all the earth's shattering rain
By allowing myself to spit these lyrics just for you

So that I may find peace of my inner man
Which enables me on my own to stand

Undefeated capturing all your words hurt
left lingering
Allowing me to spit these lyrics just for you.

Incomplete

Down blackened streets
I journey looking for my home
Lost but found still searching
answering why I feel alone
Thankful for the peace I found
yet longing to be complete
Kept for grace and mercy
connecting to souls I sit and weep
Free outside but bound inside
to a silent void that lurks within
Looking for the arms to run to
when I don't even have a friend
Lost all sense of direction
silenced by emotions web
The phones just keep on ringing
the voices echoing over and over in my head
Tangled in the tangible
bound with loosened ends
I'm incomplete in many areas
left to determine how to win.

Inside Out

For many years I've walked this earth captured
yet trying to break free
Many times almost lost my mind in attempts to find me
I've downloaded more thoughts than the Internet
could programs
And transposed more memories than the Bible could
scriptures because this is who I am
I've walked miles on jagged edged roads on the tips
of my toes
Pouring blood, sweat, and tears from my pores to
hand you a piece of my soul
And I've reached beyond the hindering barriers to
share my fear and doubt
Soaring deep down inside me and pouring my inside out

I've placed my soul at mercy's feet and my heart in the
hands of inspiration
In anticipation that I'd spark the engines of someone
else's creation
I lay down my life in my lyrics while standing on an
unknown foundation
While slowly exhaling through my mental hesitations
And I give it to you

I've hung lifeless in the balance of ridicule so that
your defects can gain peace
I've economized my mind so your blinded visions
could see
I've colonized my spirit so that my words may set
you free
So I poured my insides out and gave you a piece of me

No Name on A New Entry

On a clear canvas I eloquently designed
the script for an unspoken dream
Where nothing ever appears quite as it seems
I tell the story of the teardrops
slowly hitting my window seal
While fiction erupts into reality
and becomes what's real
I paint the script of closed legs,
still rivers and closed hearts
Of graceful guidance and lessons
taught, and a world apart
Where my children play in peace
gracefully in meadows grass
Of purple trees, red grass,
pure gold flowers, and a white past
Diamonds fresh from the mine
Freedom from strife after the passing of time
Gentle thoughts of quiet falls,
roars of thunder and melodious calls
And the nonsense of a broken down
dream behind brick walls

Misfit

Can't measure up to the expectations
Trying to be everyone else
Still searching for your own identity
The reflection you see is not even
of yourself
Everyday being judged by saved
and unsaved too
Unable to satisfy others and you can't
even please you
Too weary to step forward and
too tired to go back
Too devastated to keep going
on anybody's track
Mind always wondering you
can't ever seem to fit in
No matter what you do you're
the misfit in the end
The saved folks say they want you
and they talk about you too
The sinners can't seem to stand you
but they still welcome you
You can't have your cake let
alone eat it too
All you want is to fit in so
what are you going to do?
Cast out of your comfort zone and
you're searching for anything to grasp within
Feeling like you don't belong with nobody
else and all you wanted was a friend.

Create

Create with me a song of melody
Warm harmony played by an extraordinary symphony
On a patch of mustard seeds
Leaving just enough faith to move a mountain
As stumbling blocks fall so rapidly I just quit counting

Create with me a friendship built on trust without thorns
A life of spiritual royalty, prosperity, and treasures unborn
Opened eyes and upgraded respects
Revolving halos and tender pecks
Shared secrets on sculptured hills
Designed successes with binding seals

Create within us a vision of intertwined assets
Have untangled lyrics and moderate sets
Exquisite scenes and inattentive goals untold
Journeys traveled as tales unfold

One Mind One God

Strong in His will yet still close minded to His way
Headed in the right direction yet still stuck
Not seeing what affects, the young people today
You act as though we're saved we're limited to the moves we make
But you failed to realize it's Satan's joy not our own we set out to take

You can't keep me bound by religion when I'm trying to break free
The Bible says let everything that has breath praise the Lord and in order to do so I just gotta be me
That doesn't mean I can only dance like David danced and it doesn't mean I have to a shout
I can't sing with the angels, run, jump, and about

I am anointed in my talents therefore my anointing manifested my gifts
On my face praying when my spirit needs a lift
Striving toward a prosperous future with no dictation of my past
You think that because I'm young I don't have enough knowledge to last

But I'll make mistakes in life
I'm imperfect just like you
So don't act like you're just so holy that you have to criticize me when I'm going through
And after all my mess comes the message of how I can deliver you

So before your flesh condemns me pray that we fall on one accord
Because we are all saints serving one God, here to praise the same Lord!

A New Creation

I'm a new creation
No limitation
With no hesitation
I do what needs to be done
Until my battle is won
And I have victory and not defeat
Safe in my Savior's arms now weep
At a new creation
I look at how my life was
turned upside down
Spinning like a merry-go-round
Until a man named Jesus was found
I remember how He saved me
and set me free
Gave me hopes and dreams to see
Made my visions reality
And in the midst of a storm showed me
a sign of possibility
Now I'm a new creation
Striving to make a difference
With no hindrance
Nothing standing in my way
As I move forth to a brighter day
At my Savior's side I stay
As a new creation.

Depression

I sit in a room depressed, wondering, and waiting
Time seems to be traveling so slow,
but yet sit anticipating still waiting
With nowhere to go
Thinking about everything between
now and the past
Never knowing how long the moment will last
My head begins to ache with the pains
of the problems I endured in life
My heart throbs with the memory
of the passing of his wife
The passing of his wife
who was my only mother
And only a year later
the passing of his brother
The passing memories of my mother,
his brother,
my uncle,
his wife
The passing memories of all the stress
I endured in life
Feeling all the heartaches and pains
Almost thinking I'm going insane
But I can't stop the memory
I yearn for her guidance so much
I reach for her hand
but their memories not even I can't touch
I look for someone else
A different mother as if
But no one can replace the mother I miss!

What to Do

I look at my life and the road I'm taking
Then I slow down with caution
because of the path I've been making
Not knowing who I am
or what I want to be
Not knowing if you're mine
or if you're trying to hurt me
Yet no longer will I sit alone in a room
crying because I'm broken hearted
Feeling the pains
that someone else has started
I'm just constantly praying that I'll awaken
to see tomorrow to see the sun
Praying that I can go outside
and not feel the painful shot of a gun
Praying asking the Lord to guide me
safely through another day
Praying asking the Lord to guide me
continuously along the way
Thanking the Lord each time the mission is done
Happily singing, shouting, and rejoicing
because finally I've won!

Where I Live

Cops chasing kids cause they robbed the corner store
Families moving out cause they can't take it here no more
Adolescents smoking weed cause they think it's cool
But they just don't know they look like a fool
A brother and a sister ages four and two
Walking up and down the street with nothing to do
No one knows their parents or even where they live
So we give them what they need after all they're only kids

Dang Casey twelve smoking weed and pregnant too
And her drug-dealing boyfriend got shot and he might not make it through
Billy needs to feel some pain so he set himself on fire
Said the pains help lift his spirit higher

The lady across the street eyes are blood shot red from crying for so long
Her daughter packed her bags and got up and moved on
Rachel's funeral is tomorrow
Yep the pretty fourteen-year-old done died
Said she couldn't take it so she committed suicide
Sad to say that this is half the problems that go on from day to day
And I see it all the time cause this is where I stay!

Down Low

Up and Down
Round and Round
You slide, move, twist and turn
Passionately making love until your soul
Begins to burn

From such an incredible sensation
Without any hesitation
There's another round of continuation
And during the rising of your emotions
There's no more commotion

No regrets or confusions
There was also no protection we're using
It all happened so quick
Now your candles are no longer lit

And it was all on the down low
Nobody has to know
At least that's what you said
And look where it lead
I'm lying in a hospital bed

From one night of pleasure
Delivering your child
Man ain't this wild
And all along nobody knew
Not even you

Cause it was all on the down low

Now I'm spending an eternity in pain
Things ain't gone never be the same
My joy and happiness is no more
All my love is out of the door

But there's nothing else for me to do
I'm through messing around with you
You went to be with someone else
And I'm raising this baby by myself

But it's okay cause I'm gon' be alright
You see my future is out of sight
And this down low mess won't be racking my brain
My life will not remain the same
I got responsibilities now
And I can't let this baby go out like I went down
On the down low!

My Mind

In my mind I see you loving me and by any means necessary it's going to be
If I have to lay on my back and spread my lips
While you climb inside rotating your hips
Then so be it, but I need love from you

Even though it won't be true I can't be alone
Even though I'm on my own scared, confused, misused, and abused
I need you to love me
So I'm making this reality
By any means necessary
In my mind

In my mind I'm not worthy of the love you have to give
But I work hard to make your candle lit love live
Because I need it, I have to have it, and I can't let go
So don't say no

Don't hurt me or break my heart
Even though I see the start
Of the life I left
the hoein', the smoking, the shooting, the crime
So I wouldn't be behind
So I can stay ahead
And be worthy of the love that led
Me to the hospital bed

With bruises and scars
No more fancy cars or luxury rides

But your loves still on my side
Hanging on
In my mind

But you were just hanging around
Because you couldn't leave town
Till you knew for sure I was okay
The guilt kept you there hanging on
Knowing I was here because you were running...
Round and round, and round you went
Spreading your legs
HUSH
Open up quick
Now because of you here I stand
With a virus in my body and the grim reaper in my hand
See your love was all in my mind
All the time

But because I desired it, needed it, couldn't live without it, I didn't
And it's sad
But too bad
Because it's too late I'm gone
So long
The love in my mind

I Wasn't Assigned to You

Baby even though I'm an STD
I wasn't assigned to you, you found me
You had more run ins than a corner store and the
Seven Eleven
No protection cause you thought the sex was heaven
Now your scent is unbearable and your sores won't allow
you to sit
Because the moments of pleasure were so good to you
You didn't know when to quit

You couldn't get enough of Jim, John, James, Paul,
Anthony, Kevin, Tim, and Tyrone
Now you're walking around with crabs, syphilis,
gonorrhea, herpes, and your all alone
You took more turns than a doorknob and your news
came today
You tested HIV positive and your life has gone astray
What! You regret the decisions you made
Now you've had far more than enough
Now you want to stop, why?
Is the competition getting tough?
What's wrong are you scared?
Are your last days spent in fear?
Why now turn and run shedding tear after tear?

You chose to continuously open your legs,
I wasn't assigned to you
You came looking for me
when you chose to do what you wanted to

So here's the price you pay for trying to run in my
high price game
I not only ruined your body, but your life
cause to me it's all the same

I Never Claimed Perfect

I've never claimed a perfect life and
I never portrayed things to be
I've made many mistakes just like any other,
I'm human, I am me
Looking for love in all the wrong places
not seeing what it truly means
I looked for others to fill the void
to hand me the finer things
Talked about and ridiculed because of
the unfit choices I made
Yet woman enough to handle the consequences
that comes in the bed I laid

Attempting to redeem myself in deliverance
by turning away from man
No longer desiring to search for
what I failed to understand
By Christ I've been forgiven,
but you want my life
You want me to severely suffer
to fill me with misery and strife
Upon my grave you've placed titles
of everything you thought of me
But I've never claimed a perfect life,
LOVED is all I wanted to be

The hardest thing I ever faced was
turning away from man
Breaking down my flesh so that
on my own two feet I stand
Able to confront my mistakes

seeing just how trifling I really was
Turning my back to God
hoping you could supply my love
Hoping you could give me joy and peace
and rid me of all my pain
Stopping the cries for help in my lyrics
that were written and made plain

Instead I got more heartache, more trials,
and more defeat
At rock bottom sinking further
I THOUGHT I was in too deep
Satan had a trap set and
in my mind created his own personal playground
And every time I tried to get up
he'd push me further down

But God still made a way
when my road I could not see
When my life I could not end
and no one else did the job I was me
Imperfect in all my ways
I maintained with what I had
Now I'm being lied on in attempts to be ruined
and can't even get mad
You're quick to point the finger and shoot the blame
One faces me and three back at you
so WHAT do you possibly have to gain
I've never claimed a perfect a life
LOVED is all I ever wanted to be
I've made mistakes just like any other
I'm human, I'm only me.

Remember This

I remember the day oh so clear
It was in September of "95"
When God called my mother home
And made me open my eyes

I was my last day as a child
And as a teen I never knew
I became overpowered by so much pain
I didn't what to do

So I shut down and strayed away
From all my friends and family too
After everything else transpired
I didn't know how I would make it through

One thing after another
My problem never stopped
Every time I made it through one
There was another stumbling block

Finally, I had enough
I just couldn't take it anymore
I turned my back to things
And to life I closed the door

Three, four, five times
I tried to end my life
The pain was more than I could bare
I carried too much misery and strife

Then we had her funeral
Oh yeah I remember it loud and clear
Where so many times I saw you
And each time you were coming near

I remember watching the tears
That came streaming from your eyes
And I knew they were for me
As I screamed out in agonizing pain
Wondering... my God how could this be

I remember how you came near me
With your arms stretched open wide
And you tried to comfort me then
But frightened by your tears I ran away
And for years held everything within

Yes, I remember being a young girl then
Forced to deal with oh so much
And you often prayed me through
See I never forgot your encouraged words or gentle touch

But I also remember the mistake I made
When I cast all my painful memories away
Because I also rid myself of all the promising messages
People blessed me with that day

I also left behind a lot of my inspiration
That through the years I really longed for
I forgot about you also
Although you never closed your door

You were a friend of my mothers
And when she passed so did a piece of you and I
But I was blinded by too much pain to see that then
I was too busy continuously asking why

I just couldn't grasp the concept
That she wasn't coming back
When I found her on the living room floor
Everything left me just like that

And even though you were always available
Whenever I needed to talk
I couldn't handle the distance between us
That's why I'd always go for a walk

I would think about the words I needed
To explain just what I felt
But I could never form a conversation
To get through the problems I'd been dealt

Then many years later again our paths crossed
And as always you tried to ease my pain
You told me "Everything would be okay"
And since then things were no longer the same

I moved back and forth
Never having a place to actually call home
Never knowing who I truly was
I just felt so all alone

Now here I am a young woman
Out and on my own

And you're still around encouraging me
Not to give up and to keep pushing on

So together we keep moving
Never once letting to
Continuously jumping hurdles
Only to meet Jesus I know

So as we part I say good bye
Only to know I'll never see you again
And as long as I live
You'll have a place in my heart
Where your encouragement rests within.

Shedding the Emptiness

Shedding tears of joy
Shedding tears of sorrow
I pray for better days
I pray for peace tomorrow

Shedding tears of anger
Shedding tears of pain
In the midst of it all
I pray that I stay sane

Shedding tears of misery
Shedding tears of strife
I have faith things will get better
I pled the blood of Jesus over my life

Shedding tears of peace
Shedding tears of pleasure
Knowing I have the victory
I dry my face from stormy weather!

Alone

I fear my life's a repeat
Like nothing's going to change
I feel I have a future
Yet there's no love that will remain

I fear my loved ones will leave
I fear they'll leave me by myself
I see the repeat coming
As I'm staring at myself

I thought things would be different now
But no one has really changed
I thought they would have learned by now
But every one's still the same

I thought I could make a difference
I thought I could do it on my own
But I couldn't change the unchangeable
That's why now I'm all alone.

Broken Promises

No more broken promises
And soft spoken goodbyes
No more special moments
Resulting in heart aching cries

No more yearning for guidance
On a path that doesn't exist
No more using me as a target
On a range you never missed

No more misguided love
That ended with a closed door
No more pretended inspiration
Up on a deserted shore

No, no more broken words
That will never come true
Why? Because my mentality
Has risen above you!

www.ingramcontent.com/pod-product-compliance
Lightning Source LLC
Chambersburg PA
CBHW060342080526
44584CB00013B/890